ESSENTIAL
Pasta

p

Contents

Introduction

Pasta is one of the earliest culinary inventions and dates back as far as the second century BC. Italy and pasta may seem synonymous, however pasta-making traditions have been traced in countries other than Italy, such as China, Mongolia, Greece, Spain, Israel, and Russia.

It was commonly thought that Marco Polo brought the art of pasta-making to Italy after his travels in China. However, it is now recognised that he was already familiar with pasta before travelling to China as it was first made by the Etruscans in central Italy in 500 BC.

Regardless of its origin, pasta is now a worldwide favourite. Not only is it nutritious, it is cheap and extremely versatile too. For those with a busy lifestyle, pasta made from durum wheat which contains protein and carbohydrates, is a great energy provider and takes just a few minutes to cook.

It is a good idea to always have a supply of dried pasta, such as rigatoni, spaghetti or perhaps fusilli in your cupboard, as it can be cooked quickly and added to pasta sauce for a tasty meal. Alternatively you can buy fresh pasta from your delicatessen or local supermarket. However, be careful when choosing fresh pasta.

It is generally more expensive than the dried alternative and is usually not any better. In fact, fresh pasta often contains lower levels of protein than dried pasta and can be less absorbent and more starchy.

There are as many as 200 different types of pasta to choose from, in various shapes and sizes, and all can be combined with fish, meat, poultry, vegetables, herbs or even fruit to create delicious appetising meals.

To make a basic pasta dough at home use 450 g/1 lb/4 cups durum wheat flour, 4 lightly beaten eggs and 1 tbsp of olive oil with a pinch of salt. On a lightly floured surface, sift the flour and salt into a mound. Make a well in the middle and add the eggs and olive oil. Use a fork or your fingers to gradually work the mixture until the ingredients are combined and knead for 10–15 minutes. Set the dough aside to rest for 25 minutes, before rolling it out as thinly as possible.

Pasta should be cooked in lightly salted boiling water until it is tender yet firm to the bite. The Italians call this *al dente* (to the tooth). Dried unfilled pasta takes 8–12 minutes; fresh unfilled pasta takes 2–3 minutes; dried filled pasta takes 15–20 minutes; fresh filled pasta takes 8–10 minutes. To prevent sticking and to enhance flavour add a tablespoon of olive oil to the boiling water. Once the pasta is cooked, drain it in a colander and serve with sauce.

Minestrone

Serves 8–10

INGREDIENTS

3 garlic cloves
3 large onions
2 celery sticks (stalks)
2 large carrots
2 large potatoes
100 g/3^1/$_2$ oz French (green)
  beans
100 g/3^1/$_2$ oz courgettes
  (zucchini)
60 g/2 oz/4 tbsp butter

50 ml/2 fl oz/^{1}/$_4$ cup olive oil
60 g/2 oz rindless fatty bacon,
  finely diced
1.5 litres/2^3/$_4$ pints/6^7/$_8$ cups
  vegetable or chicken stock
100 g/3^1/$_2$ oz chopped
  tomatoes
2 tbsp tomato purée (paste)
1 bunch fresh basil, finely
  chopped

100 g/3^1/$_2$ oz Parmesan
  cheese rind
85 g/3 oz dried spaghetti,
  broken up
salt and pepper
freshly grated Parmesan
  cheese, to serve

1 Finely chop the garlic, onions, celery, carrots, potatoes, beans and courgettes (zucchini).

2 Heat the butter and oil together in a large saucepan, add the bacon and cook for 2 minutes. Add the garlic and onion and fry for 2 minutes, then stir in the celery, carrots and potatoes and fry for a further 2 minutes.

3 Add the beans to the pan and fry for 2 minutes. Stir in the courgettes (zucchini) and fry for a further 2 minutes. Cover the pan and cook all the vegetables, stirring frequently, for 15 minutes.

4 Add the stock, tomatoes, tomato purée (paste), basil, and cheese rind and season to taste. Bring to the boil,

lower the heat and simmer for 1 hour. Remove and discard the cheese rind.

5 Add the spaghetti pieces to the pan and cook for 20 minutes. Serve in large, warm soup bowls sprinkled with freshly grated Parmesan cheese.

Ravioli alla Parmigiana

Serves 4

285 g/10 oz Basic Pasta Dough
1.2 litres/2 pints/5 cups veal
   stock
freshly grated Parmesan
   cheese, to serve

FILLING:
100 g/3$^1/_2$ oz/1 cup freshly
   grated Parmesan cheese
100 g/3$^1/_2$ oz/1$^2/_3$ cups fine
   white breadcrumbs
2 eggs

125 ml/4 fl oz/$^1/_2$ cup
   Espagnole Sauce (see
   Cook's Tip, below)
1 small onion, finely chopped
1 tsp freshly grated nutmeg

1 Make the basic pasta dough. Carefully roll out 2 sheets of the pasta dough and cover with a damp tea towel (dish cloth) while you make the filling for the ravioli.

2 To make the filling, mix together the grated Parmesan cheese, white breadcrumbs, eggs, espagnole sauce (see Cook's Tip, right), chopped onion and the freshly grated nutmeg in a large mixing bowl.

3 Place spoonfuls of the filling at regular intervals on 1 sheet of pasta dough. Cover with the second sheet of pasta dough, then cut into squares and seal the edges.

4 Bring the veal stock to the boil in a large pan. Add the ravioli and cook for about 15 minutes.

5 Transfer the soup and ravioli to warm serving bowls and serve at once, generously sprinkled with Parmesan cheese.

COOK'S TIP

For espagnole sauce, melt 2 tbsp butter and stir in 25g/1 oz/$^1/_4$ cup plain flour until smooth. Stir in 1 tsp tomato purée, 250 ml/ 9 fl oz/1$^1/_8$ cups hot veal stock, 1 tbsp Madeira and 1$^1/_2$ tsp white wine vinegar. Dice 25 g/1 oz each bacon, carrot and onion and 15 g/ $^1/_2$ oz each celery, leek and fennel. Fry with a thyme sprig and a bay leaf in oil. Drain, add to the sauce and simmer for 4 hours. Strain.

Pea & Egg Noodle Soup with Parmesan Cheese Croûtons

Serves 4

INGREDIENTS

3 slices smoked, rindless, fatty
    bacon, diced
1 large onion, chopped
15 g/^{1}/$_2$ oz/1 tbsp butter
450 g/1 lb/2^1/$_2$ cups dried
    peas, soaked in cold water
    for 2 hours and drained

2.3 litres/4 pints/10 cups
    chicken stock
225 g/ 8 oz dried egg noodles
150 ml/^{1}/$_4$ pint/^{5}/$_8$ cup double
    (heavy) cream
salt and pepper

chopped fresh parsley, to
    garnish
Parmesan cheese croûtons
    (see Cook's Tip, below),
    to serve

1 Put the bacon, onion and butter in a large pan and cook over a low heat for about 6 minutes.

2 Add the peas and the chicken stock to the pan and bring to the boil. Season lightly with salt and pepper, cover and simmer for 1½ hours.

3 Add the egg noodles to the pan and simmer for a further 15 minutes.

4 Pour in the cream and blend thoroughly. Transfer to soup bowls, garnish with parsley and top with Parmesan cheese croûtons (see Cook's Tip, right). Serve immediately.

VARIATION

Use other pulses, such as dried haricot (navy) beans, borlotti or pinto beans, instead of the peas.

COOK'S TIP

To make Parmesan cheese croûtons, cut a French stick into slices. Coat each slice lightly with olive oil and sprinkle with Parmesan cheese. Grill (broil) for about 30 seconds.

Tuscan Veal Broth

Serves 4

INGREDIENTS

60 g/2 oz/^{1}/$_3$ cup dried peas, soaked for 2 hours and drained
900 g/2 lb boned neck of veal, diced
1.2 litres/2 pints/5 cups beef or brown stock (see Cook's Tip)

600 ml/1 pint/2^1/$_2$ cups water
60 g/2 oz/^{1}/$_3$ cup barley, washed
1 large carrot, diced
1 small turnip (about 175 g/6 oz), diced
1 large leek, thinly sliced

1 red onion, finely chopped
100 g/3^1/$_2$ oz chopped tomatoes
1 fresh basil sprig
100 g/3^1/$_2$ oz/^{3}/$_4$ cup dried vermicelli
salt and white pepper

1 Put the peas, veal, stock and water into a large saucepan and gently bring to the boil. Using a slotted spoon, skim off any scum that rises to the surface of the liquid.

2 When all of the scum has been removed, add the barley and a pinch of salt to the mixture. Simmer gently over a low heat for 25 minutes.

3 Add the carrot, turnip, leek, onion, tomatoes and basil to the pan, and season to taste. Simmer for about 2 hours, skimming the surface from time to time. Remove the pan from the heat and set aside for 2 hours.

4 Set the pan over a medium heat and bring to the boil. Add the vermicelli and cook for 12 minutes. Season with salt and pepper to taste and remove and discard the basil. Ladle into soup bowls and serve immediately.

COOK'S TIP

Brown stock is made with veal bones and shin of beef roasted with dripping (drippings) in the oven for 40 minutes. Transfer the bones to a pan, add sliced leeks, onion, celery and carrots, a bouquet garni, white wine vinegar and a thyme sprig and cover with water. Simmer over a very low heat for 3 hours. Strain and blot the fat from the surface with kitchen paper.

Mussel & Potato Soup

Serves 4

INGREDIENTS
---

750 g/1 lb 10 oz mussels
2 tbsp olive oil
100 g/3^1/$_2$ oz/7 tbsp unsalted
  butter
2 slices rindless, fatty bacon,
  chopped
1 onion, chopped
2 garlic cloves, crushed

60 g/2 oz/^{1}/$_2$ cup plain
  (all purpose) flour
450 g/1 lb potatoes, thinly
  sliced
100 g/3^1/$_2$ oz/^{3}/$_4$ cup
  dried conchigliette
300 ml/^{1}/$_2$ pint/1^1/$_4$ cups
  double (heavy) cream

1 tbsp lemon juice
2 egg yolks
salt and pepper

TO GARNISH:
2 tbsp finely chopped fresh
  parsley
lemon wedges

1 Debeard the mussels and scrub them under cold water for 5 minutes. Discard any mussels that do not close immediately when sharply tapped.

2 Bring a large pan of water to the boil, add the mussels, oil and a little pepper and cook until the mussels open.

3 Drain the mussels, reserving the cooking liquid. Discard any mussels that are closed. Remove the mussels from their shells.

4 Melt the butter in a large saucepan and cook the bacon, onion and garlic for 4 minutes. Stir in the flour, then 1.2 litres/ 2 pints/5 cups of the reserved cooking liquid.

5 Add the potatoes to the pan and simmer for 5 minutes. Add the conchigliette and simmer for a further 10 minutes.

6 Add the cream and lemon juice, season to taste, then add the mussels to the pan.

7 Blend the egg yolks with 1-2 tbsp of the remaining cooking liquid, stir into the pan and cook for 4 minutes.

8 Ladle the soup into 4 warm individual soup bowls, garnish with the chopped fresh parsley and lemon wedges and serve.

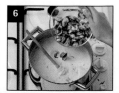

Spaghetti alla Carbonara

Serves 4

INGREDIENTS

425 g/15 oz dried spaghetti
2 tbsp olive oil
1 large onion, thinly sliced
2 garlic cloves, chopped
175 g/6 oz rindless bacon, cut
    into thin strips

25 g/1 oz/2 tbsp butter
175 g/6 oz mushrooms, thinly
    sliced
300 ml/$\frac{1}{2}$ pint/$1\frac{1}{4}$ cups
    double (heavy) cream
3 eggs, beaten

100 g /$3\frac{1}{2}$ oz/1 cup freshly
    grated Parmesan cheese,
    plus extra to serve
    (optional)
salt and pepper
fresh sage sprigs, to garnish

1 Warm a large serving dish or bowl. Bring a large pan of lightly salted water to the boil. Add the spaghetti and 1 tbsp of the oil and cook until tender, but still firm to the bite. Drain, return to the pan and keep warm.

2 Heat the remaining oil in a frying pan (skillet) over a medium heat. Add the onion and fry until it is transparent. Add the garlic and bacon and fry until the bacon is crisp. Transfer to the warm dish.

3 Melt the butter in the frying pan (skillet). Add the mushrooms and fry, stirring occasionally, for 3-4 minutes. Return the bacon mixture to the pan. Cover and keep warm.

4 Mix together the cream, eggs and cheese in a large bowl and then season to taste with salt and pepper.

5 Working very quickly, tip the spaghetti into the bacon and mushroom mixture and pour over the eggs. Toss the spaghetti quickly into the egg and cream mixture, using 2 forks. Garnish and serve with extra grated Parmesan cheese, if using.

COOK'S TIP

The key to success with this recipe is not to overcook the egg. That is why it is important to keep all the ingredients hot enough just to cook the egg and to work rapidly to avoid scrambling it.

Chorizo & Wild Mushrooms with a Spicy Vermicelli

Serves 6

INGREDIENTS

680 g/1¹/₂ lb dried vermicelli	225 g/8 oz wild mushrooms	salt and pepper
125 ml/4 fl oz/¹/₂ cup olive oil	3 fresh red chillies, chopped	10 anchovy fillets, to garnish
2 garlic cloves	2 tbsp freshly grated	
125 g/4¹/₂ oz chorizo, sliced	Parmesan cheese	

1 Bring a large pan of lightly salted water to the boil. Add the vermicelli and 1 tbsp of the oil and cook until just tender, but still firm to the bite. Drain, place on a warm serving plate and keep warm.

2 Meanwhile heat the remaining oil in a large frying pan (skillet). Add the garlic and fry for 1 minute. Add the chorizo and wild mushrooms and cook for 4 minutes, then add the chopped chillies and cook for 1 further minute.

3 Pour the chorizo and wild mushroom mixture over the vermicelli and season. Sprinkle over the freshly grated Parmesan cheese, garnish with a lattice of anchovy fillets and serve immediately.

VARIATION

Fresh sardines may be used instead of the anchovies. However, ensure that you gut and clean the sardines, removing the backbone, before using them.

COOK'S TIP

Always obtain wild mushrooms from a reliable source: never pick them yourself unless you are sure of their identity. Many varieties of mushrooms are now cultivated and most are indistinguishable from the wild varieties. Mixed colour oyster mushrooms are used here, but you could also use chanterelles. However, chanterelles shrink during cooking, so you may need more.

Orecchiette with Bacon & Tomatoes

Serves 4

INGREDIENTS

900 g/2 lb small, sweet
    tomatoes
6 slices rindless, smoked bacon
60 g/2 oz/4 tbsp butter
1 onion, chopped

1 garlic clove, crushed
4 fresh oregano sprigs,
    finely chopped
450 g/1 lb/4 cups dried
    orecchiette

1 tbsp olive oil
salt and pepper
fresh basil sprigs, to garnish
freshly grated Pecorino
    cheese, to serve

1 Blanch the tomatoes in boiling water. Drain, skin and seed the tomatoes, then roughly chop the flesh. Chop the bacon into small dice.

2 Melt the butter in a saucepan and fry the bacon until it is golden. Add the onion and garlic and fry for 5-7 minutes, until softened.

3 Add the tomatoes and oregano to the pan and season to taste. Lower the heat and simmer for 10-12 minutes.

4 Bring a pan of lightly salted water to the boil. Add the orecchiette and oil and cook for 12 minutes, until just tender, but still firm to the bite. Drain and transfer to a serving dish. Spoon over the bacon and tomato sauce and toss to coat. Garnish and serve.

VARIATION

You could also use 450 g/ 1 lb spicy Italian sausages. Squeeze the meat out of the skins and add to the pan in step 2 instead of the bacon.

COOK'S TIP

For an authentic Italian flavour use pancetta, rather than ordinary bacon. This kind of bacon is streaked with fat and adds rich undertones of flavour to many traditional dishes. It is available both smoked and unsmoked and can be bought in a single, large piece or cut into slices. You can buy it in some supermarkets and all Italian delicatessens.

Marinated Aubergine (Eggplant) on a Bed of Linguine

Serves 4

INGREDIENTS

150 ml/¹/₄ pint/⁵/₈ cup
   vegetable stock
150 ml/¹/₄ pint/⁵/₈ cup white
   wine vinegar
2 tsp balsamic vinegar
3 tbsp olive oil
fresh oregano sprig

450 g/1 lb aubergine
   (eggplant), peeled and
   thinly sliced
400 g/14 oz dried linguine

MARINADE:
2 tbsp extra virgin oil
2 garlic cloves, crushed

2 tbsp chopped fresh oregano
2 tbsp finely chopped
   roasted almonds
2 tbsp diced red (bell) pepper
2 tbsp lime juice
grated rind and juice of
   1 orange
salt and pepper

1 Put the vegetable stock, wine vinegar and balsamic vinegar into a saucepan and bring to the boil over a low heat. Add 2 tsp of the olive oil and the sprig of oregano and simmer gently for about 1 minute.

2 Add the aubergine slices to the pan, remove from the heat and set aside for 10 minutes.

3 Meanwhile, make the marinade. Combine the oil, garlic, fresh oregano, almonds, (bell) pepper, lime juice, orange rind and juice and seasoning in a large bowl.

4 Remove the aubergine (eggplant) from the saucepan with a slotted spoon, and drain well. Mix the aubergine (eggplant) slices into the marinade,

and set aside in the refrigerator for 12 hours.

5 Bring a pan of salted water to the boil. Add half the remaining oil and the linguine and cook until just tender. Drain the pasta and toss with the remaining oil. Arrange the pasta on a serving plate with the aubergine (eggplant) slices and the marinade and serve.

Gnocchi Piemontese

Serves 4

INGREDIENTS

450 g/1 lb warm mashed
    potato
75 g/2³/₄ oz/⁵/₈ cup self-
    raising (self-rising) flour
1 egg

2 egg yolks
1 tbsp olive oil
150 ml/¹/₄ pint/⁵/₈ cup
    Espagnole Sauce

60 g/2 oz/4 tbsp butter
175 g/6 oz/2 cups freshly
    grated Parmesan cheese
salt and pepper
fresh herbs, to garnish

1 Combine the mashed potato and flour in a bowl. Add the egg and egg yolks, season well and mix together to form a dough.

2 Break off pieces and roll between the palms of your hands to form small balls the size of a walnut. Flatten the balls with a fork into the shape of small cylinders.

3 Bring a pan of lightly salted water to the boil. Add the gnocchi and olive oil and poach for 10 minutes.

4 Mix the Espagnole sauce and the butter in a large saucepan over a gentle heat. Gradually blend in the grated Parmesan cheese.

5 Remove the gnocchi from the pan and toss in the sauce, transfer to individual serving plates, garnish and serve.

COOK'S TIP

This dish also makes an excellent main meal with a crisp salad.

VARIATION

These gnocchi would also taste delicious with a tomato sauce, in Trentino-style. Mix together 115 g/4 oz/ 1 cup finely chopped sun-dried tomatoes, 1 finely sliced celery stick (stalk), 1 crushed garlic clove and 6 tbsp red wine in a pan. Cook over a low heat for 15–20 minutes. Stir in 8 skinned, chopped, Italian plum tomatoes, season to taste with salt and pepper and simmer over a low heat for a further 10 minutes.

Spaghetti Bolognese

Serves 4

INGREDIENTS

3 tbsp olive oil
2 garlic cloves, crushed
1 large onion, finely chopped
1 carrot, diced
225 g/8 oz/2 cups lean minced (ground) beef, veal or chicken

85 g/3 oz chicken livers, finely chopped
100 g/3½ oz lean, Parma ham (prosciutto), diced
150 ml/¼ pint/⅝ cup Marsala

285 g/10 oz can chopped plum tomatoes
1 tbsp chopped fresh basil leaves
2 tbsp tomato purée (paste)
salt and pepper
450 g/1 lb dried spaghetti

1 Heat 2 tbsp of the olive oil in a large saucepan. Add the garlic, onion and carrot and fry for 6 minutes.

2 Add the minced (ground) beef, veal or chicken, chicken livers and Parma ham (prosciutto) to the pan and cook over a medium heat for 12 minutes, until well browned.

3 Stir in the Marsala, tomatoes, basil and tomato purée (paste) and cook for 4 minutes. Season to taste with salt and pepper. Cover and simmer for about 30 minutes.

4 Remove the lid from the pan, stir and simmer for a further 15 minutes.

5 Meanwhile, bring a large pan of lightly salted water to the boil. Add the spaghetti and the remaining oil and cook for about 12 minutes, until tender, but still firm to the bite. Drain and transfer to a serving dish. Pour the sauce over the pasta, toss and serve hot.

VARIATION

Chicken livers are an essential ingredient in a classic Bolognese sauce to which they add richness. However, if you prefer not to use them, you can substitute the same quantity of minced (ground) beef.

Creamed Strips of Sirloin with Rigatoni

Serves 4

INGREDIENTS

75 g/3 oz/6 tbsp butter	pinch of freshly grated root	PASTA:
450 g/1 lb sirloin steak,	ginger	450 g/1 lb dried rigatoni
trimmed and cut into thin	2 tbsp dry sherry	2 tbsp olive oil
strips	150 ml/¼ pint/⅝ cup double	2 fresh basil sprigs
175 g/6 oz button	(heavy) cream	115 g/4 oz/8 tbsp butter
mushrooms, sliced	salt and pepper	
1 tsp mustard	4 slices hot toast, cut into	
	triangles, to serve	

1 Melt the butter in a frying pan (skillet) and fry the steak over a low heat for 6 minutes. Transfer to an ovenproof dish and keep warm.

2 Add the mushrooms to the remaining juices in the frying pan (skillet) and cook for 2–3 minutes. Add the mustard, ginger, salt and pepper. Cook for 2 minutes, then add the sherry and cream. Cook for 3 minutes, then pour the cream sauce over the steak.

3 Bake the steak and cream mixture in a preheated oven at 90°C/ 375°F/Gas 5 for 10 minutes.

4 Bring a pan of lightly salted water to the boil. Add the rigatoni, olive oil and 1 basil sprig and boil for 10 minutes. Drain and transfer to a warm serving plate. Toss the pasta with the butter and garnish with the remaining basil sprig.

5 Serve the steak with the pasta and triangles of warm toast.

Tagliarini with Meatballs in Red Wine & Oyster Mushroom Sauce

Serves 4

INGREDIENTS

150 g/5 oz/2 cups white
  breadcrumbs
150 ml/^{1}/4 pint/^{5}/8 cup milk
225 g/8 oz/3 cups sliced
  oyster mushrooms
25 g/1 oz/2 tbsp butter
9 tbsp olive oil
25 g/1 oz/^{1}/4 cup wholemeal
  (whole-wheat) flour

200 ml/7 fl oz/^{7}/8 cup beef
  stock
150 ml/^{1}/4 pint/^{5}/8 cup red
  wine
4 tomatoes, skinned and
  chopped
1 tbsp tomato purée (paste)
1 tsp brown sugar

1 tbsp finely chopped fresh
  basil
12 shallots, chopped
450 g/1 lb/4 cups minced
  (ground) steak
1 tsp paprika
450 g/1 lb dried egg tagliarini
salt and pepper
fresh basil sprigs, to garnish

1 Soak the breadcrumbs in the milk for 30 minutes.

2 Fry the mushrooms in half the butter and 4 tbsp of the oil until soft. Stir in the flour. Add the stock and wine and simmer for 15 minutes. Add the tomatoes, tomato purée (paste), sugar and basil and simmer for 30 minutes.

3 Mix the shallots, steak and paprika with the breadcrumbs. Season then shape into 14 meatballs.

4 Heat 4 tbsp of the remaining oil and the butter in a frying pan (skillet). Fry the meatballs until brown all over. Transfer to a casserole, pour over the red wine and the mushroom sauce, cover and bake in a preheated oven at 180°C/350°F/Gas 4 for 30 minutes.

5 Bring a pan of salted water to the boil. Add the pasta and the remaining oil and cook until tender. Drain and transfer to a serving dish. Pour the meatballs and sauce on to the pasta. Garnish with fresh basil and serve.

Sicilian Spaghetti

Serves 4

150 ml/¼ pint/⅝ cup olive
oil, plus extra for brushing
2 aubergines (eggplants)
350 g/12 oz/3 cups minced
(ground) beef
1 onion, chopped
2 garlic cloves, crushed
2 tbsp tomato purée (paste)

400 g/14 oz can chopped
tomatoes
1 tsp Worcestershire sauce
1 tsp chopped fresh marjoram
or oregano or ½ tsp dried
marjoram or oregano
60 g/2 oz/½ cup stoned
(pitted) black olives, sliced

1 green, red or yellow (bell)
pepper, cored, seeded and
chopped
175 g/6 oz dried spaghetti
115 g/4 oz/1 cup freshly
grated Parmesan cheese
salt and pepper

1 Brush a 20 cm/8 inch loose-based round cake tin (pan) with oil, line the base with baking parchment and brush with oil.

2 Slice the aubergines (eggplants). Fry the aubergines (eggplants) in a little oil until browned on both sides. Drain on kitchen paper (towels).

3 Cook the beef, onion and garlic in a pan, stirring, until browned. Add the tomato purée (paste), tomatoes, Worcestershire sauce, herbs and salt and pepper. Simmer for 10 minutes. Add the olives and (bell) pepper and cook for a further 10 minutes.

4 Bring a pan of salted water to the boil. Add the spaghetti and 1 tbsp olive oil and cook until tender. Drain and turn the spaghetti into a bowl. Add the meat mixture and cheese and toss to mix.

5 Arrange aubergine (eggplant) slices over the base and sides of the tin (pan). Add the pasta, then cover with the rest of the aubergine (eggplant). Bake in a preheated oven at 200°C/400°F/ Gas 6 for 40 minutes. Leave to stand for 5 minutes, then invert on to a serving dish. Discard the baking parchment and serve.

Lasagne Verde

Serves 4–6

INGREDIENTS

butter, for greasing
14 sheets pre-cooked lasagne
850 ml/1¹/₂ pints/3³/₄ cups
    Béchamel Sauce
75 g/3 oz/³/₄ cup grated
    mozzarella cheese
fresh basil (optional), to
    garnish

MEAT SAUCE:
25 ml/1 fl oz/¹/₈ cup olive oil
450 g/1 lb/4 cups minced
    (ground) beef
1 large onion, chopped
1 celery stick (stalk), diced
4 cloves garlic, crushed
25g/1 oz/¹/₄ cup plain
    (all purpose) flour

300 ml/¹/₂ pint/1¹/₄ cups beef
    stock
150 ml/¹/₄ pint/⁵/₈ cup red
    wine
1 tbsp chopped fresh parsley
1 tsp chopped fresh marjoram
1 tsp chopped fresh basil
2 tbsp tomato purée (paste)
salt and pepper

1 To make the meat sauce, heat the olive oil in a large frying pan (skillet). Add the minced (ground) beef and fry, stirring frequently, until browned all over. Add the onion, celery and garlic and cook for 3 minutes.

2 Sprinkle over the flour and cook, stirring constantly, for 1 minute. Gradually stir in the stock and red wine. Season well

and add the parsley, marjoram and basil. Bring to the boil, lower the heat and simmer for 35 minutes. Add the tomato purée (paste) and simmer for a further 10 minutes.

3 Lightly grease an ovenproof dish with butter. Arrange sheets of lasagne over the base of the dish, spoon over a layer of meat sauce, then Béchamel Sauce. Place another layer

of lasagne on top and repeat the process twice, finishing with a layer of Béchamel Sauce. Sprinkle over the grated mozzarella cheese.

4 Bake the lasagne in a preheated oven at 190°C/375°F/Gas 5 for 35 minutes, until the top is golden brown and bubbling. Garnish with fresh basil, if liked, and serve immediately.

Pasticcio

Serves 6

INGREDIENTS

250 g/8 oz/2 cups dried fusilli
1 tbsp olive oil, plus extra
    for brushing
4 tbsp double (heavy) cream
mixed salad, to serve

SAUCE:
2 tbsp olive oil
1 onion, thinly sliced
1 red (bell) pepper, cored,
    seeded and chopped

2 garlic cloves, chopped
600 g/1 lb 5 oz/5^1/4 cups
    minced (ground) beef
400 g/14 oz can chopped
    tomatoes
125 ml/4 fl oz/^{1}/2 cup dry
    white wine
2 tbsp chopped fresh parsley
60 g/2 oz can anchovies,
    drained and chopped
salt and pepper

TOPPING:
300 ml/^{1}/2 pint/1^1/4 cups
    natural yogurt
3 eggs
pinch of freshly grated
    nutmeg
40 g/1^1/2 oz/^{1}/2 cup freshly
    grated Parmesan cheese

1 To make the sauce, heat the oil in a frying pan (skillet) and fry the onion and red (bell) pepper for 3 minutes. Add the garlic and cook for 1 minute. Add the beef and cook until browned.

2 Add the tomatoes and wine and bring to the boil. Simmer for 20 minutes, until thickened.

Stir in the parsley, anchovies and seasoning.

3 Bring a pan of salted water to the boil. Add the pasta and oil and cook for 10 minutes, until almost tender. Drain and transfer to a bowl. Stir in the cream.

4 For the topping, beat together the yogurt, eggs and nutmeg.

5 Brush an ovenproof dish with oil. Spoon in half the pasta and cover with half the meat sauce. Repeat, then spread over the topping and sprinkle with cheese.

6 Bake in a preheated oven at 190°C/375°F/ Gas 5 for 25 minutes until golden. Serve with a mixed salad.

Neapolitan Veal Cutlets with Mascarpone Cheese & Marille

Serves 4

INGREDIENTS

200 g/7 oz/⁷/₈ cup butter
4 x 250 g/9 oz veal cutlets, trimmed
1 large onion, sliced
2 apples, peeled, cored and sliced
175 g/6 oz button mushrooms

1 tbsp chopped fresh tarragon
8 black peppercorns
1 tbsp sesame seeds
400 g/14 oz dried marille
100 ml/3¹/₂ fl oz/scant ¹/₂ cup extra virgin olive oil

175 g/6 oz/³/₄ cup mascarpone cheese, broken into small pieces
salt and pepper
2 large beef tomatoes, cut in half
leaves of 1 fresh basil sprig

1 Melt 60 g/2 oz/4 tbsp of the butter in a frying pan (skillet). Gently fry the veal for 5 minutes on each side. Transfer to a dish and keep warm.

2 Fry the onion and apples until golden. Transfer to a dish, top with the veal and keep warm.

3 Fry the mushrooms, tarragon and peppercorns in the remaining butter for 3 minutes. Sprinkle over the sesame seeds.

4 Bring a pan of salted water to the boil. Add the pasta and 1 tbsp of the oil and cook until tender. Drain and transfer to a serving plate.

5 Top the pasta with the cheese and sprinkle over the remaining olive oil. Place the onions, apples and veal cutlets on top of the pasta. Spoon the mushrooms, peppercorns and pan juices on to the cutlets, place the tomatoes and basil leaves around the edge of the plate and place in a preheated oven at 150°C/300°F/Gas 2 for 5 minutes. Season to taste with salt and pepper and serve immediately.

Stuffed Cannelloni

Serves 4

INGREDIENTS

8 dried cannelloni tubes
1 tbsp olive oil
25 g/1 oz/^{1}/4 cup freshly
    grated Parmesan cheese
fresh herb sprigs, to garnish

FILLING:
25 g/1 oz/2 tbsp butter
300 g/10^1/2 oz frozen spinach,
    thawed and chopped

115 g/4 oz/1^1/2 cup ricotta
    cheese
25 g/1 oz/^{1}/4 cup freshly
    grated Parmesan cheese
60 g/2 oz/^{1}/4 cup chopped
    ham
pinch of freshly grated
    nutmeg
2 tbsp double (heavy) cream
2 eggs, lightly beaten

·salt and pepper

SAUCE:
25 g/1 oz/2 tbsp butter
25 g/1 oz/^{1}/4 cup plain
    (all purpose) flour
300 ml/^{1}/2 pint/1^1/4 cups milk
2 bay leaves
pinch of freshly grated
    nutmeg

1 For the filling, melt the butter in a pan and stir-fry the spinach for 2–3 minutes. Remove from the heat and stir in the cheeses and the ham. Season with nutmeg, salt and pepper. Beat in the cream and eggs to make a thick paste.

2 Cook the pasta with the oil in a pan of salted boiling water until tender. Drain and set aside.

3 To make the sauce, melt the butter in a pan. Stir in the flour and cook for 1 minute. Gradually stir in the milk and the bay leaves and simmer for 5 minutes. Add the nutmeg and seasoning. Remove from the heat and discard the bay leaves.

4 Spoon the filling into a piping bag and fill the cannelloni.

5 Spoon a little sauce into the base of an ovenproof dish. Arrange the cannelloni in the dish in a single layer and pour over the remaining sauce. Sprinkle over the Parmesan cheese and bake in a preheated oven at 190°C/375°F/Gas 5 for about 40–45 minutes. Garnish with the fresh herb sprigs and serve immediately.

Tagliatelle with Pumpkin

Serves 4

INGREDIENTS

500 g/1 lb 2 oz pumpkin or
butternut squash, peeled
and seeded
3 tbsp olive oil
1 onion, finely chopped
2 garlic cloves, crushed
4–6 tbsp chopped fresh
parsley

pinch of freshly grated
nutmeg
about 250 ml/9 fl oz/1¹/₄ cups
chicken or vegetable stock
115 g/4 oz Parma ham
(prosciutto)
250 g/9 oz dried tagliatelle

150 ml/¹/₄ pint/⁵/₈ cup double
(heavy cream)
salt and pepper
freshly grated Parmesan
cheese, to serve

1 Cut the pumpkin or butternut squash in half and scoop out the seeds. Cut the flesh into 1 cm/½ inch dice.

2 Heat 2 tbsp of the olive oil in a large saucepan and fry the onion and garlic over a low heat for about 3 minutes, until soft. Add half the parsley and fry for 1 minute.

3 Add the pumpkin or squash pieces and cook

for 2–3 minutes. Season to taste with salt, pepper and nutmeg.

4 Add half the stock to the pan, bring to the boil, cover and simmer for 10 minutes, or until the pumpkin or squash is tender, adding more stock if necessary.

5 Add the Parma ham (prosciutto) to the pan and cook, stirring frequently, for 2 minutes.

6 Bring a large pan of lightly salted water to the boil. Add the tagliatelle and the remaining oil and cook for 12 minutes, until tender, but still firm to the bite. Drain and transfer to a warm serving dish.

7 Stir the cream into the pumpkin and ham mixture and heat through. Spoon over the pasta, sprinkle over the remaining parsley and serve immediately.

Tagliatelle with Chicken Sauce

Serves 4

INGREDIENTS

250 g/9 oz fresh green
   tagliatelle
1 tbsp olive oil
fresh basil leaves, to garnish
salt

TOMATO SAUCE:
2 tbsp olive oil
1 small onion, chopped
1 garlic clove, chopped

400 g/14 oz can chopped
   tomatoes
2 tbsp chopped fresh parsley
1 tsp dried oregano
2 bay leaves
2 tbsp tomato purée (paste)
1 tsp sugar
salt and pepper

CHICKEN SAUCE:
60 g/2 oz/4 tbsp unsalted
   butter
400 g/14 oz boned chicken
   breasts, skinned and cut
   into thin strips
90 g/3 oz/^{3}/4 cup blanched
   almonds
300 ml/^{1}/2 pint/1^1/4 cups
   double (heavy) cream
salt and pepper

1 To make the tomato
   sauce, heat the oil and
fry the onion until
translucent. Add the garlic
and fry for 1 minute. Stir
in the tomatoes, herbs,
tomato purée (paste), sugar
and seasoning to taste.
Bring to the boil and
simmer for 15–20 minutes,
until reduced by half.
Remove from the heat and
discard the bay leaves.

2 To make the chicken
   sauce, melt the butter
in a frying pan (skillet) and
stir-fry the chicken and
almonds for 5–6 minutes,
until the chicken is cooked.

3 Meanwhile, bring the
   cream to the boil over
a low heat for about 10
minutes, until reduced by
half. Pour the cream over
the chicken and almonds,

stir and season to taste.
Set aside and keep warm.

4 Bring a pan of salted
   water to the boil. Add
the tagliatelle and olive oil
and cook until tender.
Drain and transfer to a
warm serving dish. Spoon
over the tomato sauce and
arrange the chicken sauce
on top. Garnish with the
basil leaves and serve.

Tortellini

Serves 4

INGREDIENTS

115 g/4 oz boned chicken breast, skinned	pinch of ground allspice	SAUCE:
60 g/2 oz Parma ham (prosciutto)	1 egg, beaten	300 ml/¹/₂ pint/1¹/₄ cups single (light) cream
40 g/1¹/₂ oz cooked spinach, well drained	450 g/1 lb Basic Pasta Dough	2 garlic cloves, crushed
1 tbsp finely chopped onion	salt and pepper	115 g/4 oz button mushrooms, thinly sliced
2 tbsp freshly grated Parmesan cheese	2 tbsp chopped fresh parsley, to garnish	4 tbsp freshly grated Parmesan cheese

1 Bring a pan of seasoned water to the boil. Add the chicken and poach for 10 minutes. Cool slightly, then process in a food processor, with the Parma ham (prosciutto), spinach and onion until finely chopped. Stir in the Parmesan cheese, allspice and egg and season to taste.

2 Thinly roll out the pasta dough and cut into 5 cm/2 inch rounds.

3 Place ¹/₂ tsp of the filling in the centre of each round. Fold the pieces in half and press the edges to seal. Then wrap each piece around your index finger, cross over the ends and curl the rest of the dough backwards to make a navel shape.

4 Bring a pan of salted water to the boil. Add the tortellini, bring back to the boil and cook for

5 minutes. Drain and transfer to a serving dish.

5 To make the sauce, bring the cream and garlic to the boil then simmer for 3 minutes. Add the mushrooms and half the cheese, season and simmer for 2–3 minutes. Pour the sauce over the tortellini. Sprinkle over the remaining Parmesan, garnish with the parsley and serve.

Chicken with Green Olives & Pasta

Serves 4

INGREDIENTS

4 chicken breasts, part boned
3 tbsp olive oil
25 g/1 oz/2 tbsp butter
1 large onion, finely chopped
2 garlic cloves, crushed
2 red, yellow or green (bell)
   peppers, cored, seeded and
   cut into large pieces

250 g/9 oz button
   mushrooms, sliced or
   quartered
175 g/6 oz tomatoes, skinned
   and halved
150 ml/$\frac{1}{4}$ pint/$\frac{5}{8}$ cup dry
   white wine

175 g/6 oz/1$\frac{1}{2}$ cups stoned
   (pitted) green olives
4–6 tbsp double (heavy) cream
400 g/14 oz dried pasta
salt and pepper
chopped parsley, to garnish

1 Fry the chicken breasts in 2 tbsp of the oil and the butter until golden brown. Remove the chicken from the pan.

2 Add the onion and garlic to the pan and fry until beginning to soften. Add the (bell) peppers and mushrooms and cook for 2–3 minutes. Add the tomatoes and seasoning. Transfer the vegetables to a casserole with the chicken.

3 Add the wine to the pan and bring to the boil. Pour the wine over the chicken. Cover and cook in a preheated oven at 180°C/350°F/Gas 4 for 50 minutes.

4 Mix the olives into the casserole. Pour in the cream, cover and return to the oven for 10–20 minutes.

5 Meanwhile, bring a large pan of lightly salted water to the boil. Add the pasta and the remaining oil and cook until tender, but still firm to the bite. Drain the pasta well and transfer to a serving dish.

6 Arrange the chicken on top of the pasta, spoon over the sauce, garnish with the parsley and serve immediately. Alternatively, place the pasta in a large serving bowl and serve separately.

Sliced Breast of Duckling
with Linguine

Serves 4

INGREDIENTS
---

4 x 275 g/10^1/$_2$ oz boned
  breasts of duckling
25 g/1 oz/2 tbsp butter
50 g/2 oz/3^3/$_8$ cups finely
  chopped carrots
50 g/2 oz/4 tbsp finely
  chopped shallots
1 tbsp lemon juice

150 ml/^{1}/$_4$ pint/^{5}/$_8$ cup meat
  stock
4 tbsp clear honey
115 g/4 oz/^{3}/$_4$ cup fresh or
  thawed frozen raspberries
25 g/1 oz/^{1}/$_4$ cup plain (all
  purpose) flour
1 tbsp Worcestershire sauce

400 g/14 oz fresh linguine
1 tbsp olive oil
salt and pepper

TO GARNISH:
fresh raspberries
fresh sprig of flat-leaf parsley

---

1 Trim and score the duck breasts and season well. Melt the butter in a frying pan (skillet) and fry the duck breasts until lightly coloured.

2 Add the carrots, shallots, lemon juice and half the meat stock and simmer for 1 minute. Stir in half the honey and half the raspberries. Stir in half

the flour and cook for 3 minutes. Add the pepper and Worcestershire sauce.

3 Stir in the remaining stock and cook for 1 minute. Stir in the remaining honey, raspberries and flour. Cook for a further 3 minutes.

4 Remove the duck from the pan, but continue simmering the sauce.

5 Bring a large pan of salted water to the boil. Add the linguine and olive oil and cook until tender. Drain and divide between 4 plates.

6 Slice the duck breast lengthways into 5 mm/^{1}/$_4$ inch thick pieces. Pour a little sauce over the pasta and arrange the sliced duck in a fan shape on top. Garnish and serve.

Rigatoni & Pesto Baked Partridge

Serves 4

INGREDIENTS

8 partridge pieces
(about 115 g/4 oz each)
60 g/2 oz/4 tbsp butter, melted
4 tbsp Dijon mustard
2 tbsp lime juice

1 tbsp brown sugar
6 tbsp Pesto Sauce
450 g/1 lb dried rigatoni
1 tbsp olive oil

115 g/4 oz/1^{1}/3 cups freshly
grated Parmesan cheese
salt and pepper

1 Arrange the partridge pieces, smooth side down, in a single layer in a large, ovenproof dish.

2 Mix together the butter, Dijon mustard, lime juice and brown sugar in a bowl. Season to taste. Brush the mixture over the upper surfaces of the partridge pieces and bake in a preheated oven at 200°C/400°F/Gas 6 for 15 minutes.

3 Remove the dish from the oven and coat the partridge pieces with 3 tbsp of the Pesto Sauce. Return to the oven and bake for a further 12 minutes.

4 Remove the dish from the oven and carefully turn over the partridge pieces. Coat the top of the partridges with the remaining mustard mixture and return to the oven for a further 10 minutes.

5 Meanwhile, bring a large saucepan of lightly salted water to the boil. Add the rigatoni and olive oil and cook for about 10 minutes until tender, but still firm to the bite. Drain and transfer to a serving dish. Toss the pasta with the remaining Pesto Sauce and the Parmesan.

6 Arrange the pieces of partridge on the serving dish with the rigatoni, pour over the cooking juices and serve immediately.

VARIATION

You could also prepare young pheasant in the same way.

Cannelloni Filetti di Sogliola

Serves 6

INGREDIENTS

12 small fillets of sole
(about 115 g/4 oz each)
150 ml/^{1}/$_4$ pint/^{5}/$_8$ cup red
wine
90 g/3 oz/6 tbsp butter
115 g/4 oz/3^7/$_8$ cups sliced
button mushrooms

4 shallots, finely chopped
115 g/4 oz tomatoes, chopped
2 tbsp tomato purée (paste)
60 g/2 oz/^{1}/$_2$ cup plain (all
purpose) flour, sifted
150 ml/^{1}/$_4$ pint/^{5}/$_8$ cup of
warm milk

2 tbsp double (heavy) cream
6 dried cannelloni tubes
175 g/6 oz cooked, peeled
prawns (shrimp), preferably
freshwater
salt and pepper
1 fresh dill sprig, to garnish

1 Brush the fillets with a little wine. Season and roll up, skin side inwards. Secure with a skewer or cocktail stick (toothpick).

2 Arrange the fish rolls in a single layer in a large frying pan (skillet), add the remaining red wine and poach for 4 minutes. Remove from the pan and reserve the cooking liquid.

3 Melt the butter in another pan. Fry the mushrooms and shallots for 2 minutes, then add the tomatoes and tomato purée (paste). Season the flour and stir it into the pan. Stir in the reserved cooking liquid and half the milk. Cook over a low heat, stirring, for 4 minutes. Remove from the heat and stir in the cream.

4 Bring a pan of salted water to the boil. Add the cannelloni and cook for 8 minutes, until tender but still firm to the bite. Drain and set aside to cool.

5 Remove the skewers or cocktail sticks from the fish rolls. Put 2 sole fillets into each cannelloni tube with 3–4 prawns (shrimp) and a little red wine sauce. Arrange the cannelloni in an ovenproof dish, pour over the sauce and bake in a preheated oven at 200°C/ 400°F/ Gas 6 for 20 minutes.

6 Serve the cannelloni with the red wine sauce, garnished with a sprig of dill.

Red Mullet Fillets with Orecchiette, Amaretto & Orange Sauce

Serves 4

INGREDIENTS

90 g/3 oz/3³/4 cup plain (all purpose) flour
8 red mullet fillets
25 g/1 oz/2 tbsp butter
150 ml/¹/4 pint/⁵/8 cup fish stock
1 tbsp crushed almonds
1 tsp pink peppercorns

1 orange, peeled and cut into segments
1 tbsp orange liqueur
grated rind of 1 orange
450 g/1 lb dried orecchiette
1 tbsp olive oil
150 ml/¹/4 pint/⁵/8 cup double (heavy) cream

4 tbsp amaretto
salt and pepper

TO GARNISH:
2 tbsp snipped fresh chives
1 tbsp toasted almonds

1 Season the flour and sprinkle into a shallow bowl. Press the fish fillets into the flour to coat. Melt the butter in a frying pan (skillet) and fry the fish over a low heat for 3 minutes, until browned.

2 Add the fish stock to the pan and cook for 4 minutes. Carefully remove the fish, cover with foil and keep warm.

3 Add the almonds, pink peppercorns, half the orange, the orange liqueur and orange rind to the pan. Simmer until the liquid has reduced by half.

4 Meanwhile, bring a large saucepan of lightly salted water to the boil. Add the orecchiette and olive oil and cook for 15 minutes, until tender but still firm to the bite.

5 Season the sauce and stir in the cream and amaretto. Cook for 2 minutes. Coat the fish with the sauce in the pan.

6 Drain the pasta and transfer to a serving dish. Top with the fish fillets and their sauce. Garnish with the remaining orange segments, the chives and toasted almonds. Serve.

Spaghetti al Tonno

Serves 4

INGREDIENTS

200 g/7 oz can tuna, drained	60 g/2 oz/1 cup roughly	450 g/1 lb dried spaghetti
60 g/2 oz can anchovies,	chopped flat leaf parsley,	25 g/1 oz/2 tbsp butter
drained	plus extra to garnish	salt and pepper
250 ml/9 fl oz/1⅛ cups	150 ml/¼ pint/⅝ cup crème	black olives, to garnish
olive oil	fraîche	crusty bread, to serve

1 Remove any bones from the tuna. Put the tuna into a food processor or blender, together with the anchovies, 225 ml/8 fl oz/1 cup of the olive oil and the flat leaf parsley. Process until smooth.

2 Spoon the crème fraîche into the food processor or blender and process again for a few seconds to blend thoroughly. Season to taste.

3 Bring a large pan of lightly salted water to the boil. Add the spaghetti and the remaining olive oil and cook until tender, but still firm to the bite.

4 Drain the spaghetti, return to the pan and place over a medium heat. Add the butter and toss well to coat. Spoon in the sauce and quickly toss into the spaghetti, using 2 forks.

5 Remove the pan from the heat and divide the spaghetti between 4 warm individual serving plates. Garnish with olives and parsley and serve with warm, crusty bread.

VARIATION

If liked, you could add 1–2 garlic cloves to the sauce, substitute 25 g/ 1 oz/½ cup chopped fresh basil for half the parsley and garnish with capers instead of black olives.

Spaghetti with Smoked Salmon

Serves 4

INGREDIENTS

450 g/1 lb dried buckwheat
    spaghetti
2 tbsp olive oil
90 g/3 oz/$\frac{1}{2}$ cup crumbled
    feta cheese
salt

fresh coriander (cilantro) or
    parsley leaves, to garnish

SAUCE:
300 ml/$\frac{1}{2}$ pint/1$\frac{1}{4}$ cups
    double (heavy) cream
150 ml/$\frac{1}{4}$ pint/$\frac{5}{8}$ cup whisky
    or brandy

125 g/4$\frac{1}{2}$ oz smoked salmon
pinch of cayenne pepper
black pepper
2 tbsp chopped fresh coriander
    (cilantro) or parsley

1 Bring a large pan of lightly salted water to the boil. Add the spaghetti and 1 tbsp of the olive oil and cook until tender, but still firm to the bite. Drain and return to the pan with the remaining olive oil. Cover, set aside and keep warm.

2 Pour the cream into a small saucepan and bring to simmering point, but do not let it boil. Pour the whisky or brandy into another small saucepan and bring to simmering point, but do not allow it to boil. Remove both pans from the heat and mix together the cream and whisky or brandy.

3 Cut the smoked salmon into thin strips and add to the cream mixture. Season with cayenne and black pepper. Just before serving, stir in the fresh coriander (cilantro) or parsley.

4 Transfer the spaghetti to a warm serving dish, pour over the sauce and toss thoroughly with 2 large forks. Scatter over the crumbled feta cheese, garnish with the coriander (cilantro) or parsley leaves and serve immediately.

COOK'S TIP

Serve this rich and luxurious dish with a green salad tossed in a lemony dressing.

Trout with Pasta Colle Acciughe & Smoked Bacon

Serves 4

INGREDIENTS
---

4 x 275 g/9^1/$_2$ oz trout, gutted
   and cleaned
12 anchovies in oil, drained
   and chopped
2 apples, peeled, cored and
   sliced
4 fresh mint sprigs

juice of 1 lemon
12 slices rindless, smoked,
   fatty bacon
butter, for greasing
450 g/1 lb dried tagliatelle
1 tbsp olive oil
salt and pepper

TO GARNISH:
2 apples, cored and sliced
4 fresh mint sprigs

1 Open up the cavities of each trout and wash with warm salt water.

2 Season each cavity with salt and black pepper. Divide the anchovies, sliced apples and mint sprigs between each of the cavities. Sprinkle the lemon juice into each cavity.

3 Carefully cover the whole of each trout, except the head and tail, with three slices of smoked bacon in a spiral.

4 Arrange the trout on a deep, greased baking (cookie) sheet with the loose ends of bacon tucked underneath. Season with black pepper and bake in a preheated oven at 200°C/400°F/Gas 6 for about 20 minutes, turning the trout over after 10 minutes.

5 Bring a large pan of salted water to the boil. Add the tagliatelle and oil and cook for about 12 minutes, until tender but still firm to the bite. Drain and transfer to a warm serving dish.

6 Remove the trout from the oven and arrange on the tagliatelle. Garnish with sliced apples and fresh mint sprigs and serve immediately.

Saffron Mussel Tagliatelle

Serves 4

| INGREDIENTS |

1 kg/2¼ lb mussels
150 ml/¼ pint/⅝ cup white
    wine
1 medium onion, finely
    chopped
25 g/1 oz/2 tbsp butter
2 garlic cloves, crushed

2 tsp cornflour (cornstarch)
300 ml/½ pint/1¼ cups
    double (heavy) cream
pinch of saffron threads or
    saffron powder
1 egg yolk
juice of ½ lemon

450 g/1 lb dried tagliatelle
1 tbsp olive oil
salt and pepper
3 tbsp chopped fresh parsley,
    to garnish

1 Scrub and debeard the mussels under cold running water. Discard any that do not close when sharply tapped. Put the mussels in a pan with the wine and onion. Cover and cook over a high heat until the shells open.

2 Drain and reserve the cooking liquid. Discard any mussels that are still closed. Reserve a few mussels for the garnish and remove the remainder from their shells.

3 Strain the cooking liquid into a saucepan. Bring to the boil and reduce by about a half. Remove from the heat.

4 Melt the butter in a saucepan and fry the garlic for 2 minutes, until golden brown. Stir in the cornflour (cornstarch) and cook, stirring, for 1 minute. Gradually stir in the cooking liquid and the cream. Crush the saffron threads and add to the pan. Season to taste and simmer over a low heat for 2–3 minutes, until thickened.

5 Stir in the egg yolk, lemon juice and shelled mussels. Do not allow the mixture to boil.

6 Bring a pan of salted water to the boil. Add the pasta and oil and cook until tender. Drain and transfer to a serving dish. Add the mussel sauce and toss. Garnish with the parsley and reserved mussels and serve.

Baked Scallops with Pasta in Shells

Serves 4

INGREDIENTS

12 scallops	150 ml/^{1}/$_4$ pint/^{5}/$_8$ cup fish	225 g/8 oz/2 cups grated
3 tbsp olive oil	stock	Cheddar cheese
350 g/12 oz/3 cups small,	1 onion, chopped	salt and pepper
dried wholemeal (whole-	juice of 2 lemons	lime wedges, to garnish
wheat) pasta shells	150 ml/^{1}/$_4$ pint/^{5}/$_8$ cup double	crusty brown bread, to serve
	(heavy) cream	

1 Remove the scallops from their shells. Scrape off the skirt and the black intestinal thread. Reserve the white part (the flesh) and the orange part (the coral or roe). Carefully ease the flesh and coral from the shell with a short, but very strong knife.

2 Wash the shells thoroughly and dry them well. Put the shells on a baking (cookie) sheet, sprinkle lightly with about two thirds of the olive oil and set aside.

3 Meanwhile, bring a large saucepan of lightly salted water to the boil. Add the pasta shells and remaining olive oil and cook for about 12 minutes, until tender, but still firm to the bite. Drain and spoon about 25 g/1 oz of pasta into each scallop shell.

4 Put the scallops, fish stock and onion in an ovenproof dish and season to taste with pepper. Cover with foil and bake in a preheated oven at 180°C/350°F/Gas 4 for 8 minutes.

5 Remove the dish from the oven. Remove the foil and, using a slotted spoon, transfer the scallops to the shells. Add 1 tbsp of the cooking liquid to each shell, drizzle with lemon juice and a little cream, and top with grated cheese.

6 Increase the oven temperature to 230°C/450°F/Gas 8 and return the scallops to the oven for 4 minutes. Serve the scallops in their shells with crusty brown bread and butter.

Patriotic Pasta

Serves 4

| INGREDIENTS |

| 460 g/1 lb/4 cups dried farfalle | 460 g/1 lb cherry tomatoes | salt and pepper |
| 4 tbsp olive oil | 90 g/3 oz rocket (arugula) | Pecorino cheese, to garnish |

1 Bring a large saucepan of lightly salted water to the boil. Add the farfalle and 1 tbsp of the olive oil and cook until tender, but still firm to the bite. Drain the farfalle thoroughly and return to the pan.

2 Cut the cherry tomatoes in half and trim the rocket (arugula).

3 Heat the remaining olive oil in a large saucepan. Add the tomatoes and cook for 1 minute. Add the farfalle and the rocket (arugula) and stir gently to mix. Heat through and season to taste with salt and black pepper.

4 Meanwhile, using a vegetable peeler, shave thin slices of Pecorino cheese.

5 Transfer the farfalle and vegetables to a warm serving dish. Garnish with the Pecorino cheese shavings and serve immediately.

COOK'S TIP

Pecorino cheese is a hard sheep's milk cheese which resembles Parmesan and is often used for grating over a variety of dishes. It has a sharp flavour and is only used in small quantities.

COOK'S TIP

Rocket (arugula) is a small plant with irregular-shaped leaves rather like those of turnip tops (greens). The flavour is distinctively peppery and slightly reminiscent of radish. It has always been popular in Italy, both in salads and for serving with pasta and has recently enjoyed a revival in Britain and the United States, where it has now become very fashionable.

Linguine with Braised Fennel

Serves 4

INGREDIENTS

6 fennel bulbs
150 ml/¼ pint/⅝ cup
  vegetable stock
25 g/1 oz/2 tbsp butter

6 slices rindless, smoked
  bacon, diced
6 shallots, quartered
25 g/1 oz/¼ cup plain (all
  purpose) flour

7 tbsp double (heavy) cream
1 tbsp Madeira
450 g/1 lb dried linguine
1 tbsp olive oil
salt and pepper

1 Trim the fennel bulbs, then gently peel off and reserve the first layer of the bulbs. Cut the bulbs into quarters and put them in a large saucepan, together with the vegetable stock and the reserved outer layers. Bring to the boil, lower the heat and simmer for 5 minutes.

2 Using a slotted spoon, transfer the fennel to a large dish. Discard the outer layers of the fennel bulb. Bring the vegetable stock to the boil and allow to reduce by half. Set aside.

3 Melt the butter in a frying pan (skillet). Add the bacon and shallots and fry for 4 minutes. Add the flour, reduced stock, cream and Madeira and cook, stirring constantly, for 3 minutes, until the sauce is smooth. Season to taste and pour over the fennel.

4 Bring a large saucepan of lightly salted water to the boil. Add the linguine and olive oil and cook for 10 minutes, until tender but still firm to the bite. Drain and transfer to a deep ovenproof dish.

5 Add the fennel and sauce and braise in a preheated oven at 180°C/ 350°F/Gas 4 for 20 minutes. Serve immediately.

COOK'S TIP

Fennel will keep in the salad drawer of the refrigerator for 2–3 days, but it is best eaten as fresh as possible. Cut surfaces turn brown quickly, so do not prepare it too much in advance of cooking.

Baked Aubergines (Eggplants) with Pasta

Serves 4

INGREDIENTS

---

225 g/8 oz dried penne or
    other short pasta shapes
4 tbsp olive oil, plus extra for
    brushing
2 aubergines (eggplants)
1 large onion, chopped

2 garlic cloves, crushed
400 g/14 oz can chopped
    tomatoes
2 tsp dried oregano
60 g/2 oz mozzarella cheese,
    thinly sliced

25 g/1 oz/^{1}/$_3$ cup freshly
    grated Parmesan cheese
2 tbsp dry breadcrumbs
salt and pepper
salad leaves (greens), to serve

---

1 Bring a pan of salted water to the boil. Add the pasta and 1 tbsp of the olive oil and cook until tender. Drain, return to the pan, cover and keep warm.

2 Cut the aubergines (eggplants) in half lengthways and score around the inside, being careful not to pierce the shells. Scoop out the flesh then brush the insides of the shells with oil. Chop the flesh and set aside.

3 Fry the onion in the remaining oil until translucent. Add the garlic and fry for 1 minute. Stir in the chopped aubergine (eggplant) and fry for 5 minutes. Add the tomatoes, oregano and seasoning. Bring to the boil and simmer for 10 minutes. Remove from the heat and stir in the pasta.

4 Brush a baking (cookie) sheet with oil and arrange the aubergine (eggplant) shells in a single layer. Divide half the tomato and pasta mixture between them. Sprinkle over the mozzarella, then pile the remaining tomato and pasta mixture on top. Mix the Parmesan cheese and breadcrumbs and sprinkle over the top.

5 Bake in a preheated oven at 200°C/400°F/ Gas 6 for 25 minutes, until golden brown. Serve with salad leaves (greens).

Baked Sweet Ravioli

Serves 4

INGREDIENTS

PASTA:
425 g/15 oz/3³/₄ cups plain
  (all purpose) flour
140 g/ 5 oz/10 tbsp butter,
  plus extra for greasing
140 g/ 5 oz/³/₄ cup caster
  (superfine) sugar
4 eggs

25 g/1 oz yeast
125 ml/4 fl oz warm milk

FILLING:
175 g/6 oz/²/₃ cup chestnut
  purée
60 g/2 oz/¹/₂ cup cocoa
  powder

60 g/2 oz/¹/₄ cup caster
  (superfine) sugar
60 g/2 oz/¹/₂ cup chopped
  almonds
60 g/2 oz/1 cup crushed
  amaretti biscuits (cookies)
175 g/6 oz/⁵/₈ cup
  orange marmalade

1 To make the sweet pasta dough, sift the flour into a mixing bowl, then mix in the butter, sugar and 3 eggs.

2 Mix the yeast and warm milk in a small bowl until well combined, then mix into the dough.

3 Knead the dough for 20 minutes, cover with a clean cloth and set aside in a warm place for 1 hour to rise.

4 Combine the chestnut purée, cocoa powder, sugar, almonds, crushed amaretti biscuits (cookies) and orange marmalade in a separate bowl.

5 Grease a baking (cookie) sheet.

6 Lightly flour the work surface (counter). Roll out the pasta dough into a thin sheet and cut into 5 cm/2 inch rounds with a plain pastry cutter.

7 Put a spoonful of filling on to each round and then fold in half, pressing the edges to seal. Arrange on the prepared baking (cookie) sheet, spacing the ravioli out well.

8 Beat the remaining egg and brush all over the ravioli to glaze. Bake in a preheated oven at 180°C/350°F/Gas 4 for 20 minutes until golden. Serve hot.

German Noodle Pudding

Serves 4

INGREDIENTS

60 g/2 oz/4 tbsp butter, plus
   extra for greasing
175 g/6 oz ribbon egg noodles
115 g/4 oz/$^{1}/_{2}$ cup cream
   cheese
225 g/8 oz/1 cup cottage
   cheese

90 g/3 oz/$^{1}/_{2}$ cup caster
   (superfine) sugar
2 eggs, lightly beaten
125 ml/4 fl oz/$^{1}/_{2}$ cup soured
   cream
1 tsp vanilla essence (extract)
a pinch of ground cinnamon

1 tsp grated lemon rind
25 g/1 oz/$^{1}/_{4}$ cup flaked
   (slivered) almonds
25 g/1 oz/$^{3}/_{8}$ cup dry
   white breadcrumbs
icing (confectioners') sugar,
   for dusting

1 Grease an ovenproof dish with butter.

2 Bring a large pan of water to the boil. Add the noodles and cook until almost tender. Drain and set aside.

3 Beat together the cream cheese, cottage cheese and caster (superfine) sugar in a mixing bowl. Beat in the eggs, a little at a time, until well combined. Stir in the soured cream, vanilla

essence (extract), cinnamon and lemon rind, and fold in the noodles to coat. Transfer the mixture to the prepared dish and smooth the surface.

4 Melt the butter in a frying pan (skillet). Add the almonds and fry, stirring constantly, for about 1–1½ minutes, until lightly coloured. Remove the frying pan (skillet) from the heat and stir the breadcrumbs into the almonds.

5 Sprinkle the almond and breadcrumb mixture over the pudding and bake in a preheated oven at 180°C/350°F/Gas 4 for 35-40 minutes, until just set. Dust with a little icing (confectioners') sugar and serve immediately.

VARIATION

Although not authentic, you could add 3 tbsp raisins with the lemon rind in step 3, if liked.

Honey & Walnut Nests

Serves 4

INGREDIENTS

225 g/8 oz angel hair pasta	115 g/4 oz/^{1}/2 cup sugar	salt
115 g/4 oz/8 tbsp butter	115 g/4 oz/^{1}/3 cup clear honey	Greek-style yogurt, to serve
175 g/6 oz/1^1/2 cups shelled	150 ml/^{1}/4 pint/^{5}/8 cup water	
pistachio nuts, chopped	2 tsp lemon juice	

1 Bring a large saucepan of salted water to the boil. Add the angel hair pasta and cook until tender, but still firm to the bite. Drain the pasta and return to the pan. Add the butter and toss to coat. Set aside to cool.

2 Arrange 4 small flan or poaching rings on a baking (cookie) sheet. Divide the angel hair pasta into 8 equal quantities and spoon 4 of them into the rings. Press down lightly. Top the pasta with half of the nuts, then add the remaining pasta.

3 Bake in a preheated oven at 180°C/350°F/Gas 4 for 45 minutes, until golden brown.

4 Meanwhile, put the sugar, honey and water in a saucepan and bring to the boil over a low heat, stirring constantly until the sugar has dissolved completely. Simmer for 10 minutes, add the lemon juice and simmer for a further 5 minutes.

5 Using a palette knife (spatula), carefully transfer the angel hair nests to a serving dish. Pour over the honey syrup, sprinkle over the remaining nuts and set aside to cool completely before serving. Serve with the Greek-style yogurt.

COOK'S TIP

Angel hair pasta is also known as capelli d'Angelo. Long and very fine, it is usually sold in small bunches that already resemble nests.

This is a Parragon Book
First published in 1999
Parragon
Queen Street House
4 Queen Street
Bath BA1 1HE, UK

ISBN: 0-75253-353-3

Printed in China

Note

Cup measurements in this book are for American cups. Tablespoons are assumed to be
15 ml. Unless otherwise stated, milk is assumed to be full fat, eggs are medium and
pepper is freshly ground black pepper.